Cyntha Jarrell Massey

THE POWER OF DETERMINATION

Family History StoryBooks

Did You Like this Book?
Let us tell YOUR story!
Come visit us at familyhistorystorybooks.com and we can turn your own treasured stories into a children's book

SCAN ME

Cyntha grew up on a beautiful plantation in West Virginia filled with tall trees and clear streams. The land was like a giant garden, with apple, peach, and nut trees everywhere. Corn and sugar cane grew so high they practically touched the sky, and bees buzzed happily around their hives. This place was a paradise for a young girl like Cyntha.

Cyntha's family, the Jarrells, were strong Christians. They believed Sundays were for rest and worship, so every Saturday was busy with cooking and baking. Their pantry would be full of meats, vegetables, pies, cookies, and fruits, ready for Sunday's feast. No guest ever left their home hungry on Sundays!

Cyntha learned the value of dedication and sacrifice at a young age. She and her siblings walked four and a half miles to school every day, crossing creeks on small logs. Sometimes, Cyntha would slip into the creek and get soaked! In the winter she would often arrive at school with her clothes frozen. She was determined to learn, even if it meant spending the day near the warm stove to dry off.

Cyntha's mother often went to the mill, where she met John D. Massey, a kind mill worker who gave her extra flour. Cyntha first saw John riding a beautiful horse and thought he was the most handsome man she'd ever seen. Later, her mother introduced them and they began spending lots of time together.

In 1879, Cyntha married John. Their wedding was a beautiful, simple ceremony, filled with love and joy. It was a special day, marking the beginning of their life together. They built a little cabin and started farming and raising chickens.

They had a happy marriage, though Cyntha had to work on keeping her fiery temper under control. One day, a chicken hopped onto the dinner table and pecked at the butter. John threw the butter out the window, making Cyntha very angry. In a fit of temper, she threw dishes and even a stone jar at John!

In 1885, Latter-day Saint missionaries first arrived in town. Cyntha wanted to invite them over, but John didn't want any 'horse-thieving Mormons' to come by. Then, their baby Lewis fell very ill. The missionaries happened to knock on the door at that time, and offered to bless Lewis, promising he would get better. Miraculously, Lewis recovered immediately.

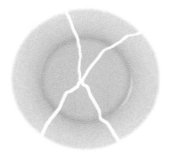

The missionaries taught the restored gospel to the Massey family, as well as other friends and family members. One night after many months of study, Cyntha's brother and John decided they would not go to sleep until they determined if the message were true. They studied and debated long into the night before deciding to go to bed and be baptized in the morning.

They were baptized in the icy waters of Joe's Creek later that same day, December 15, 1886. It took Cyntha another two months to determine for herself that this was the correct path, but after making the decision she never looked back. Their little cabin became a place for local church meetings, and a place for the missionaries to stay when they were in town.

When Cyntha and John joined the Church, some neighbors didn't like it. Once, an angry mob came to their house, wanting to harm the missionaries. Bravely, John and Cyntha stood with guns, ready to protect their guests. The mob eventually left, knowing the Masseys would not be intimidated. Cyntha's fiery determination to do what she thought was right was put to good use.

Another evening when a mob came to harm the missionaries at the Massey home, the missionaries fasted and prayed for safety. John and Cyntha prepared to defend them. But as the mob approached, a huge thunderstorm broke out, with lightning and dark clouds. Scared, the mob turned back. The missionaries' prayers for safety were answered.

After much persecution for their new faith, they decided to move out West. Cyntha became very sick following the birth of her daughter, Lois Viola. Cyntha's brother rode twenty miles to bring the missionaries so they could give her a blessing. They blessed Cyntha and she was instantly healed, and was strong enough to travel with her family to a new home.

The Masseys, along with other Saints, gathered at the train station to wait for the train to take them West. When the train pull in however, their leader felt a spiritual prompting that they shouldn't board it. They took the next train and later saw the first train had crashed. Following that spiritual prompting had saved them from a terrible accident.

When the Masseys first arrived in Southwestern Colorado, the land looked bare and tough. Cyntha worried about how they would survive. She raised chickens and sold eggs, but times were hard. They barely had enough to eat, but she never gave up. She worked hard to grow food and care for her family.

Cyntha continued to have trouble with her fiery temper! One night, their cow, Old Whitey kicked over the milk bucket. Cyntha got so mad she shot the cow with a shotgun! John fixed Old Whitey up, and the cow was fine. Although Cyntha's temper was famous and she worked to keep it under control throughout her life, her stubborn determination also made it possible for her family to survive difficult times.

Cyntha and John eventually had a large family of fifteen children, plus three they adopted! They always opened their home and hearts to those in need, creating a loving and busy household filled with laughter and life.

One of Cyntha and John's greatest wishes was to visit the Salt Lake Temple. In 1905, they traveled there and had their children sealed to them in a special ceremony. It was a dream come true, strengthening their faith and family bond.

Cyntha suffered from severe seizures as she got older. She decided that she should stop drinking coffee and live the Word of Wisdom. She prayed for help with her decision. After she quit coffee, her seizures stopped, and she never had them again. Her faith and determination helped her overcome this challenge.

Late in her life, Cyntha had a scary encounter with a sheep at her son Arthur's ranch. The sheep knocked her down twice before she managed to escape. Although she broke her leg, Cyntha didn't let it stop her. She continued working and caring for her family, showing her incredible strength and willpower.

Several years later disaster struck when a fire started in the Massey's home at Dry Fork. It burned everything they had, including their beloved organ. Fortunately, no one was hurt in the blaze. They lost almost all their possessions, but they didn't lose hope. They stayed strong and rebuilt their home, proving their resilience.

After the fire, the Masseys' life improved. Their new home had fruit trees and natural springs- just like where Cyntha grew up. She made delicious jams, sauerkraut, and root beer. John took care of beehives and opened a butcher shop. They worked hard, and their home was full of hard work and happiness.

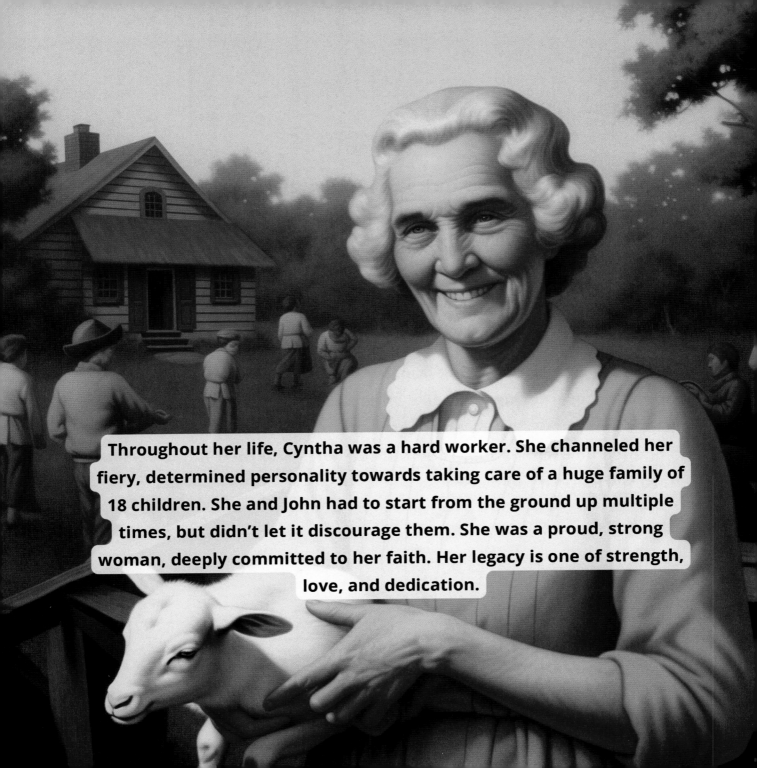

Throughout her life, Cyntha was a hard worker. She channeled her fiery, determined personality towards taking care of a huge family of 18 children. She and John had to start from the ground up multiple times, but didn't let it discourage them. She was a proud, strong woman, deeply committed to her faith. Her legacy is one of strength, love, and dedication.

Cyntha Jarrell Massey

A MOTHER TO ALL
APRIL 17, 1864 - DECEMBER 13, 1957

My Relationship:

FamilySearch.org ID: KWZQ-79H

Book Created by Cyntha's Great-Great-Great Grandson,
Jake Harmer

Order More Copies at familyhistorystorybooks.com

Family History StoryBooks

Massey Family in 1897

Undated Massey Family Photo, likely around 1901

Massey Family in 1911

Cyntha Francis Jarrell Massey

Made in the USA
Las Vegas, NV
10 October 2024